THE
ABSOLUTELY
FRIGHTFUL
JOKE BOOK

THE
ABSOLUTELY
FRIGHTFUL
JOKE BOOK

COMPILED BY
DAVID BROWN

MICHAEL O'MARA BOOKS LTD

First published in Great Britain in 1998
by Michael O'Mara Books Limited
9 Lion Yard
Tremadoc Road
London SW4 7NQ

A CIP catalogue record for this book is available from the British Library

ISBN 1-85479-419-1

1 3 5 7 9 10 8 6 4 2

Cover design by Design 23

Designed and typeset by Design 23

Printed and bound by WSOY, Finland

ABSOLUTELY FRIGHTFUL DIRTY JOKES

Two sperm are swimming along and one is beginning to get tired. He asks his friend, "How far do you think it is to the uterus? I'm getting pretty tired."

His friend says, "I'm not sure, but I think it must be a long way yet – we've only just passed the oesophagus."

Two women on a business trip were sharing a hotel room. The first night, after the lights were out, one of them came over to the other's bed and started to caress her shoulder.

"There's something I want to tell you, and I don't know how to say it, so I'll just be frank ..." Rising from her bed, the other woman interrupted, "No, I'll be Frank."

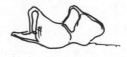

An old man, staring mournfully at his cock, intoned: "We were born together. We grew up together. We got married together. Why, oh why, did you have to die before me?"

A notice in the bedroom of an Italian hotel:
'Do not adjust your light hanger. If you wish to have it off the manageress will oblige you.'

A man was walking along the road when he saw a ladder going into the clouds. As any of us would, he started to climb the ladder. He reached a fluffy white cloud, upon which sat a rather plump and very ugly woman.

"Have sex with me or climb the ladder to success," she said.

No contest, thought the man and he climbed the ladder to the next cloud. On this cloud was a slightly thinner woman, who was rather easier on the eye.

"Make love to me or climb the ladder to success," she said. "Well," thought the man, "I might as well carry on."

On the next cloud was an even nicer woman who, this time, was quite attractive.

"Have sex with me now or climb the ladder to success," she said in gentle tones..

But he turned her down and went on up the ladder.

He thought to himself that the women were actually getting better the further up the ladder he went.

On the next cloud was an absolute beauty. Slim, attractive, the lot!

"Take me here and now or climb the ladder to success," she said.

Imagining what gorgeous creature would be waiting next, and being a gambling man, he decided to climb again.

When he reached the next cloud, there was an enormously fat ugly man, covered in hair, with flies buzzing around his head.

"Who are you?" the man asked.

"Hello" said the ugly fat man, "I'm Cess!"

A truck driver came upon a couple making passionate love in the middle of the road. He almost jumped out of his skin with fright.

He blew his horn, blinked his lights and yet the couple didn't miss a stroke!

The driver stopped, got out and shouted at them, "Are you crazy, didn't you hear my horn, see my lights, didn't you know I was coming?"

The excited young man said, "Yes, I knew you were coming! I knew she was coming and I knew I was coming! I also knew you were the only one here with brakes!"

Two old ladies were sitting on a bench together in Miami, both smoking cigarettes. One of the old ladies took out a condom and put it on her cigarette.

The other old lady looked at her and asked her why on earth she was doing that. The other old lady replied that it was supposed to be a safer way to smoke.

The next day the first old lady went to a pharmacy and asked the assistant for a condom. The assistant asked her what colour and she replied that it didn't matter.

Then the assistant asked her what size condom she needed and she said,

"I want one that will fit a Camel."

Pierre, the brave French fighter pilot, takes his girlfriend, Marie, out for a pleasant little picnic by the River Seine.

It's a beautiful day and love is in the air. Marie leans over to Pierre and says: "Pierre, my cheri, kiss me!"

Our hero grabs a bottle of Merlot and splashes it on Marie's lips. "What are you doing, Pierre?", says the startled Marie.

"I am Pierre the fighter pilot! When I have red meat, I like to have red wine!"

She smiles and they start kissing. When things began to get a little passionate, Marie says, "Pierre, kiss me lower down."

Our hero tears her blouse open, grabs a bottle of Chardonnay and starts pouring it all over her breasts.

"Pierre! What are you doing?" asks the bewildered Marie.

"I am Pierre the fighter pilot! When I have white meat, I like to have white wine!"

They resume their passionate interlude and things really get steamy!. Marie leans close to his ear and whispers, "Pierre, kiss me lower down!"

Our hero rips off her underwear, grabs a bottle of Cognac and pours it in her lap. He then strikes a match and sets the Cognac alight.

Marie shrieks and dives into the river. Standing waist deep, Marie throws her arms upwards and screams furiously,

"PIERRE, WHAT IN THE HELL DO YOU THINK YOU'RE DOING?"

Our hero stands up, defiantly, and says, "I am Pierre the fighter pilot! When I go down, I go down in flames!"

A young man talked his 90-year old father into going to a nursing home.

"It's clean, friendly, you'll meet people your own age, they'll take care of you and I won't have to worry about you being alone." said the son.

So the old man decided to try it out for a week. The very first morning he woke up with an erection. A beautiful nurse came into his room and noticed this. So she took her clothes off and made love to him. When the nurse had finished she put her clothes back on and left with a cheerful wave.

The old man called his son on the phone:

"Son! This place is wonderful! I'm so glad you talked me into this. I'm never going to leave, I want to die here!"

After he spoken to his son the old man put on his dressing gown and slippers and walked down the corridor wearing a big smile. He was so excited that he wasn't paying attention.

Suddenly he slipped and fell flat on his face.

A male orderly saw this and rushed over to him. Then he lifted up the back of the old man's dressing gown and proceeded to have passionate sex with him.

The old man was too frail to resist. When the orderly had finished the old man crawled back to his room, reached for the phone and called his son:

"Help me, son! This place is killing me! You've got to get me out of here right away. I'm going to die here!"

The son says: "Hold on dad, only 20 minutes ago you were saying how much you liked it! Now all of a sudden you've changed your mind. What's been happening?"

After explaining the sequence of events that morning the old man says: "You see son, my problem is, I only get an erection once a year but I fall down three times a day."

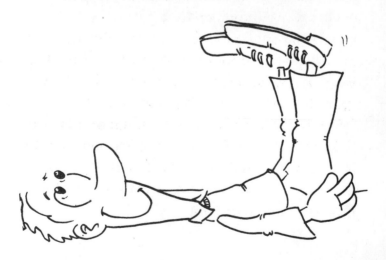

A Philadelphia truck driver is driving down the road, when he sees a large sign that says CLOCKS.

He pulls over to the side of the road, runs into the store, whips his cock out and slams it on the counter.

Calmly, the store attendant explains,

"Sorry, sir, the sign outside says CLOCKS, not COCKS."

The truck driver says, "Yes. I know – just put two hands and a face on it, and I'll be happy!"

A young woman bought a mirror at an antique shop, and placed it on her bathroom door. One evening, while getting undressed, she laughingly said,

"Mirror, mirror, on my door, make my bust-size forty-four."

Instantly, there was a brilliant flash of light, and her breasts grew to really splendid proportions.

Excitedly, she ran to tell her husband what had happened, and in minutes they both returned.

The husband crossed his fingers and said, "Mirror, mirror on the door, make my cock touch the floor!"

Again, there was a bright flash ...... and both his legs fell off.

Three men were sleeping in the same bed. In the morning they started discussing their dreams.

The man on the right said, "I had a dream that I was getting a hand job."

The man on the left said, "I had a dream that I was getting a hand job too."

Then the man in the middle said,

"That's really weird, I had a dream that I was skiing."

A 92-year-old woman and a 94-year-old man lived in a nursing home. They had been 'special' friends for five years.

Every night they would get into bed together. She would take his cock in her hand and just hold it.

They would fall asleep happily this way.

One day as the old lady was walking through the home she came across her gentleman friend in bed with another woman.

She was thoroughly distraught and screamed at him, "I've been sleeping with you for five years and now you betray me! What does she have that I don't?"

The old man replied, "Parkinsons."

A man was travelling through the Arizona desert when he came upon an Indian lying on the ground stark naked, with an erection sticking straight up in the air.

He asked the Indian what he was doing, and the Indian replied, "I'm telling the time."

The man told the Indian that he didn't believe him, so the Indian told him that it was 1:00 p.m.

The man looked at his watch and was completely amazed to find that it was, indeed, exactly 1:00 p.m.

He travelled a bit further on until he came upon yet another naked Indian lying on the ground, with an erection sticking straight up.

He asked this Indian what he was doing and he, too, replied that he was telling the time. He asked the Indian to prove it, and the Indian told him that it was exactly 2:00 p.m.

The man looked at his watch and once again is astonished to find that the time was correct.

He continued his trek through the desert until he came across an Indian lying naked in the sand, rubbing his cock. He said to this Indian, "And what the hell are you doing?"

To which the Indian replied, "I'm winding my watch."

There was this man who had a girlfriend he loved so much, he had her name tattooed on his cock.

When unaroused all you could see were the letters WY.

One day he was in a public toilet when a big black guy came up to use the urinal next to him.

Being a bit curious he looked down and, to his amazement, saw the letters WY tattooed on the other guy's cock.

"Hey, I have a tattoo just like that, is your girlfriend's name Wendy as well?"

"Nah, mine says 'Welcome to Jamaica, have a nice day', that's all." replied his neighbour with a big smile.

One day a man decided to go for a ride in his van. He was going nowhere in particular, and then he saw what seemed to be a very pretty nun walking down the road. He pulled over to pick her up and she gratefully accepted the lift, having walked over a mile already. As soon as she climbed into the van the man asked her a question that came into his mind.

"How do you nuns do that?" he asked.

"Do what?" she said.

"Manage to live with not having sex all those years?"

"I've been a nun for 25 years and I haven't done it yet, but now that you mention it, I suddenly realize I do want to."

The man was totally overcome with the same urge, so they climbed into the back of the van.

He agreed to have sex with her so that she could still be tested as a virgin. As soon as they climbed back into the front of the van, the man sighed and said, "I have a confession to make, I'm happily married with three kids."

The nun then said, "I have a confession to make, too! My name is really Harry and I'm on my way to a fancy-dress party."

Once upon a time there was a girl named Cinderella, who lived with her wicked step-mother and three step-sisters. When Prince Charming held a grand ball to find his true beloved, the wicked step-mother refused to let Cinderella go.

Alone and helpless, Cinderella could only cry silently.

Then suddenly her fairy godmother turned up. From various bits and pieces that Cinderella picked up around the house, the fairy godmother gave her everything she needed for the ball.

A collection of rags and various knick-knacks were turned into a beautiful ball gown and some of the world's best jewellery. Mice were turned into prancing white horses. A large pumpkin was turned into a coach.

The two old cats were turned into a groom and a footman.

"Oh, thank you, fairy godmother, but I just have one small problem." Cinderella confided that she was in the middle of having her period.

Looking around, they saw that there is nothing left in the house but there was a watermelon in the garden. The fairy godmother promptly turned this into a tampon.

"....and that is how Cinderella died at the stroke of midnight, Your Honour."

BLESS ME, FATHER!

A young man went into the pharmacy to buy condoms. The assistant told him that the condoms came in packs of 3, 9 or 12 and asked which the young man wanted.

"Well", he said, "I've been seeing this girl for quite a while and she's really sexy. I want the condoms because I think tonight's going to be THE night. We're having dinner with her parents, and then we're going out.

Once she's had sex with me, she'll want me all the time, so I think you'd better give me the 12-pack."

The young man bought the condoms and went home.

Later that evening, he sat down to dinner with his girlfriend and her parents. Much to his girlfriend's surprise, he asked if he might give the blessing, and her parents agreed.

He began to say grace, but carried on praying for several minutes. The girl leaned over to him and said, "You never told me that you were such a religious person."

He leaned over to her and whispered,

"You never told me that your father is a pharmacist!"

There were three men who died and went to heaven. The first man went up to see God who said, "You have committed adultery so I'm giving you a push-bike."

The second man went up and God said,

"You have almost committed adultery so I'm giving you a motorcycle."

The third man went up and God said to him,

"You have only thought about adultery, so you'll get a Porsche!"

The first man came up to the man in the Porsche and started laughing, so the man in the Porsche asked,

"Why are you laughing at me? You only got a push-bike!"

The man on the push-bike replied,

"I just saw your wife on a skateboard!"

Two nuns were riding a bike down a road and the first nun said, "I've never come this way before!"

The second nun replied, "Oh, it must be the cobblestones!"

A local vicar was paying a visit to one of his church members on a Friday night, and heard a loud party in progress as he approached the house.

He knocked on the door and the owner answered.

Behind him, he saw a circle of naked men, with blindfolded women moving from man to man. They were fondling each man's cock and guessing who it belonged to.

The vicar, seeing this, said, "I'm sorry, I don't think I'd fit in here at the moment"

"Nonsense," the man replied, "Your name's been called three times already!"

It was time for Father John's Saturday night bath and young Sister Magdalene had prepared the bath water and towels just the way the old nun had instructed.

Sister Magdalene was also told never to look at Father John's naked body if she could help it, to do whatever he told her and to pray constantly.

The next morning the old nun asked Sister Magdalene how the Saturday night bath had gone.

"Oh, sister," said the young nun dreamily. "I've been saved."

"Saved? And how did that fine thing come about?" asked the old nun.

"Well, when Father John was soaking in the bath, he asked me to wash him and, while I was washing him, he guided my hand down between his legs, where he said the Lord keeps the Key to Heaven."

"Did he now?" said the old nun evenly.

Sister Magdalene continued, "And Father John said that if the Key to Heaven fitted my lock, the portals of Heaven would be opened to me and I would be assured of salvation and eternal peace.

And then Father John guided his Key to Heaven into my lock."

"Is that a fact?" said the old nun even more evenly.

"At first it hurt terribly, but Father John said the pathway to salvation was often painful and that the glory of God would soon swell my heart with ecstasy. And so it did! It felt so good, being saved."

"That wicked old Devil," said the old nun. "He told me it was Gabriel's Horn, and I've been blowing it for 40 years!"

Priest: "Do you shrink from making love?"
Girl: "If I did, I'd be a midget!"

To me a woman's body is a temple – and I try to attend services as often as possible.

ABSOLUTELY FRIGHTFUL GOLF JOKES

For several months, Jenny had been nagging her husband Bob to take her to the country club so she could learn to play golf. He finally agreed, and off she went with a set of clubs. That afternoon, Jenny walked into the bar, grimacing with pain.

"So, did you enjoy your game of golf?" Bob asked.

"It was horrible," Jenny replied. "I got stung by a bee."

"Where?"

"Between the first and second holes," she said.

"Sounds to me," Bob replied, "like your stance was too wide."

•

Mike and Jane were beginning a game of golf

Jane stepped up to the tee, and her first drive gave her a hole in one. Mike stepped up to the tee and said, "OK, now I'll take my practice swing, and then we'll start the game"

•

"It's true," the weekend golfer told his wife on his way out of the door, "I love golf more than I love you. But," he proclaimed, "I love you more than tennis."

A husband and wife are playing golf together when one day they come upon a par 4 hole. The husband hooked his drive deep into the woods and proclaimed that he would have to chip it out.

"Maybe not, dear! said his wife. "Do you see that barn over there, if I open both doors on both sides, I do believe that you could hit it right through and onto the green!" So the husband agrees to give it a try, but when he hits the ball, it goes straight through the first doors but hits the crossbeam and ricochets back, hitting his wife and killing her.

About a year later he is playing a round on the same course with a fellow member and hooks the ball deep into the woods again. Just as he is about to chip the ball out, his partner rushes up to him and says "Do you see that barn over there? If I open both doors on both sides, I do believe that you could hit it right through and onto the green!" "No way," replies the man, sadly, "I tried that last year and got a seven!"

Colin Robinson was a rather henpecked husband. In fact, the only time he managed to get away from it all was at the annual school reunion where, each year, a trophy was awarded to the man who told the funniest story about making love to his wife. This particular year, Colin won it and proudly took the trophy home.

"What did you win that for?" demanded his wife.

"Er, it was, er... it was for telling a story about when we played golf on holiday last summer, dear," Colin stammered in reply.

"Hurrumph," grunted his wife and wandered off. The next day she bumped into the wife of another man who had been at the reunion dinner.

"Hello, Mrs Robinson," said the woman. "I gather that your Colin won a prize for telling the best story at the dinner last night."

"Yes, but I've no idea why," replied Mrs Robinson. "We only did it once. His cap blew off, he couldn't get it in the hole and he lost the ball."

Wife to Husband: "How did your golf game go today, dear?"

Husband to Wife: "Fine. I played with our dentist, Dr Blackmore."

Wife back to Husband: "Oh, that's nice. How does he play?"

Husband back to Wife: "He plays well enough, except he has this annoying habit of continually walking over to the cup on each green and saying "Would you open a little wider please?"

Arthur and Bob were playing a round of golf the other day and, just as they were about to tee off, a funeral procession went by.

Arthur put his club down, took off his cap and bowed his head as the cortège passed.

"That was a very decent gesture," said Bob.

And Arthur responded, "It was the least I could do. She was a damned good wife to me."

Wife: "You think so much about golf all the time, I bet you don't even remember when we got married."

Husband: "Of course I do, dear. It was the day I sank that twelve-yard putt."

"I haven't seen my husband for ten years," the wife said.

"Be patient," advised her lawyer. "Maybe he's taken up golf."

First man: "My wife told me this morning that if I don't give up golf she'll leave me.

Second man: "That's bad luck."

First man: "I know, I'm really going to miss her.

When Jayne's husband arrives home from the golf course several hours late, she demands an explanation.

"We had a problem," he said. "Ken collapsed and died on the second hole and from then on it was play the ball, drag Ken, play the ball, drag Ken..."

Through the first four holes of the golf course, Bob was very quiet. Finally, on the fifth tee, Barry asked, "What on earth's the matter, Bob? You haven't said one word."

"It's my wife," Bob replied. "Ever since she's been working overtime at the phone company, she's cut our sex down to twice a week."

"You're lucky," replied Barry. "She's cut me off completely."

"Shut up, Judy!" shouted the angry golfer at his nagging wife. "Shut up or you'll drive me out of my mind!"

"That wouldn't be a drive," snapped Judy in reply, "that would just be a putt."

As they left the church on the way to the reception, the groom turned to his bride saying, "I've got a confession to make, darling, I adore golf. I eat, sleep and breathe golf. I'm totally obsessed with golf and I have to tell you that it completely dominates my life."

The bride smiled sweetly at him and said, "Thank you for being so honest with me. Now, I also have something important to tell you – I'm a hooker."

"No problem," the groom replied, taking hold of her wrists. "You hold your left hand just a little higher than the right, with your thumb down here . . . . "

A young golfer was about to get married and two days before the happy event, he was hit in the groin really hard by a golf ball.

"Sorry, son," his doctor told him, "but your tackle will have to go in a splint."

On his wedding night, his young bride strips off and points at her breasts. "Aren't they beautiful?" she asks him, "and never touched by human hands."

The young man pulled down his underpants and, pointing at his crotch, says, "That's nothing, mine hasn't even been unpacked."

"So, how did it go at the golf course today?" the man asked his heavily-pregnant wife as she came in the door.

"It went great," she replied. "I played so well that when I walked off the eighteenth green, I actually felt the baby applaud.

After dessert, the women stayed around the kitchen table to chat, while the men went into the living room to talk. Soon the conversation in the living room turned to the subject of golf.

"What was your best score?" one of the men asked another.

"Let me find out," he said, as he got up and started to head towards the kitchen.

"Where are you going?" the others asked him.

"To find my wife," he replied. "She's the only one who remembers what I've been telling people."

There was a hold – up at the short eleventh hole and just as they were about to play off, a man rushed off the tenth green.

"Excuse me," he called out, "but would you mind very much if I played through? I've just heard that my wife has been taken seriously ill."

When the golfer returned home after his long day out on the links, his wife asked, "How did it go today, Bill?"

"Well, I was great at hitting the woods, for what it's worth," Bill replied.

"That's excellent, darling, well done!" she exclaimed.

"Yes, really well done," Bill said sarcastically, "now all I've got to do is learn how to hit out of them!

Mike and his secretary were having an affair. One day they decided to leave the office early and go to the secretary's flat for an afternoon of lovemaking. Afterwards, they fell asleep and didn't wake up until 8pm. They quickly got dressed and Mike asked his secretary to take his shoes and go and rub them in the grass. The secretary thought this was pretty weird, but she did it anyway.

When Mike finally arrived home his wife was waiting for him at the front door. She was clearly very upset and asked him where he had been.

Mike replied, "I cannot tell a lie. I'm having an affair with my secretary. We left work early, went to her place, made love all afternoon, and then we fell asleep. That's why I'm late!"

His wife looked at him, noticed the grass stains on his shoes and said, "You lying bastard. You've been playing golf again, haven't you?"

Chris came home one day from playing in his local golf tournament. "How did it go today?" his wife asked as he came through the door.

"Not very well, I'm afraid, Ian had to be taken off to hospital in an ambulance."

"Heavens! Chris, that's awful! What happened?"

"He was having a rotten day." said Chris. "He kept missing shot after shot and the more he missed the more angry he got. Finally, he got himself into such a state that he ruptured a blood vessel and passed out completely."

"That's really terrible," said his wife.

"I know it is," said Chris. "It gives a whole new meaning to the term 'Stroke play.'"

The day after her husband's untimely death, the widow, Mrs MacDonald met with the funeral director.

"What would you like to say in the obituary?" he enquired.

"MacDonald died." she replied.

"Don't you think that's a bit abrupt, Mrs. MacDonald?" the funeral director queried. "Isn't there anything else you might like to add?"

"Oh, all right," she said, "How about, 'Macdonald died. Golf clubs for sale.'

A husband and wife were on the ninth fairway at their local club, about to hit their approach shots to the green, when all of a sudden out of the blue, a golf ball came whizzing past them, missing the husband's head by a fraction of an inch. A minute or two later, a woman came over from the next fairway looking to retrieve her ball.

"Are you mad?" said the wife. "You hit a lousy shot like that and you don't even have the courtesy to shout 'Fore.' You know, you almost hit my husband!"

"I'm so terribly sorry." the woman apologised, holding her club out to the wife. "Here, do take a shot at mine."

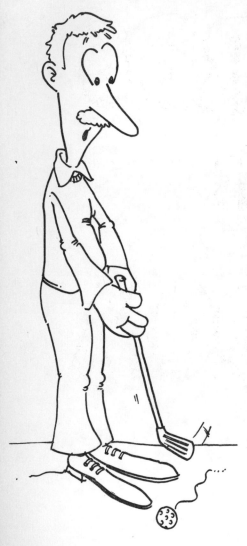

"I'm absolutely sick to death of being left alone every weekend while you go out and play golf," grumbled the golf widow to her husband one fine morning during breakfast.

"If you think you're going off to play again today, you've got another think coming!"

"Don't be ridiculous, darling," replied her husband.

"Trust me when I tell you that golf is the last thing on my mind. Let's just finish this argument once and for all. Oh, and would you mind passing the putter?"

WORDS

OF

WISDOM

Explorer: "There we were surrounded. Fierce savages everywhere you looked. They uttered awful cries and beat their clubs on the ground..."

Weary listener: "Golfers, probably."

Andy Johnson was walking on the golf course one day when he was struck on the head by a golf ball. Angrily, he demanded £500 compensation from the golfer who had driven the shot.

"But I said 'fore'," said the golfer.

"Done," said Andy.

An old man was watching a game of golf for the first time.

"What do you think of it?" asked his friend.

"It looks to me," he replied, "like a harmless little ball chased by men too old to chase anything else."

He plays a fair game of golf - if you watch him.

A golf ball is a golf ball no matter how you putt it.

Messing up yet another shot, the golfer whimpered, "There can't be worse players than me."

"There are," his partner assured him, "but they're not playing any more."

Last week I missed a spectacular hole - in - one – by only five strokes.

Golf is OK. It makes some of the best people take showers.

You can always tell the golfer who's winning. He's the one who keeps telling his opponent that it's only a game.

A shipwrecked golfer had made the best of his tiny island. When a cruise liner spotted his distress signals and sent a boat to investigate, the landing party was amazed to find a crude but recognizable nine-hole course which the castaway had played with driftwood woods, whalebone and coral putter and balls carved out of pumice stone.

"That's quite a layout," remarked the officer in charge of the landing party.

"You're very kind. It's rather basic," the rags-clad golfer responded. Then he smiled slyly and added, "But I am quite proud of the water hazard..."

Definition of a golf ball: A small object that remains on the tee while a perspiring citizen fans it vigorously with a large club.

Did you hear about the golfer who killed the Puerto Rican?

He shot a hole in Juan.

Nothing counts in a golf game like your opponent.

Golf is a lot of walking, broken up by disappointment and bad arithmetic.

Very proud of having walked around the course with him for the first time, Daddy's Little Sweetheart couldn't wait to tell everyone about her experience. "My Daddy is the best golfer in the whole world," she proclaimed. "He can play for hours and hours and hardly ever lets the ball go into one of those little holes."

When ground rules permit a golfer to improve his lie, he can either move his ball or change the story about his score.

Q: What should you do with your asshole before you have sex?
A: Drop him off at the golf club.

The headmaster was presiding at his school's Sports Day, while a celebrity guest waited to present the prizes. The head droned on through his standard set of clichés about the parallels between sport and adult life awaiting his pupils. Sportsmanship was precious, he said, and would earn success and respect in every sort of job, just as it did in any sport the boys could imagine.

"Obviously not a golfer," thought the VIP.

Two friends were sitting at the bar one evening talking about the sports they liked to play.

"I love to play golf," the first man said. "I think it's the best sport."

"No way," said his friend.

"I have a big problem with golf. There's something about it that's just not natural."

"Not natural?" the first man said. "Golf not natural? How on earth could you possibly say something like that?"

"The way I see it," said his friend, "is that there's something just not quite right about a game where the person who gets the most hits, loses!"

The difference between learning to play golf and learning to drive a car is that in golf you never hit anything.

Joe sliced his tee shot way off into a field beside the golf course. Finally, he found the ball nestled in some buttercups. On his back swing he heard a voice say, "Please don't hurt my buttercups." Joe stopped his swing, looked around, saw no one, and prepared to hit again. "Please don't hurt my buttercups," came the voice again. He stopped again, looked up and saw a beautiful woman approaching. "I am Mother Nature," she said. "If you promise not to harm my buttercups, I can guarantee an abundant supply of butter for the rest of your life."

Joe thought for a moment or two and said, "Where were you last week when I hit the ball into the pussywillows?"

His victim had been caught off guard and drawn into some serious–money betting. The golf hustler moved into top gear and started playing like a master. Aware of the dupe's suspicion, the hustler feigned surprise at his own miraculously improved form, shrugged modestly and muttered, "Somebody up there must like me."

"I hope so," snapped the burly sucker, holding his driver in a menacing manner, "because if I lose, you're likely to meet Him."

Two friends were having a drink in the clubhouse discussing equipment when the subject of woods came up.

"In my view the best wood in my bag is my five wood– it's got me out of trouble more times than I care to remember," said the first golfer.

"Oh no, I have to disagree," said his friend. "The best wood in my bag has got me out of more trouble than all the five woods on the planet ever could."

"Which wood is that?" the first man asked.

"My pencil!"

The hacker met his playing partners on the first tee.

"What's your handicap?" one of the men asked.

"My golf game!"

Two friends who hadn't seen each other for a while bumped into each other at the local golf course.

"Hi!" said the first friend, "You're looking great - have you lost weight?"

"Well, thanks for noticing," said the second friend. "I have, actually. I've been on that new golf diet. Perhaps you've heard about it?"

"No, as a matter of fact I haven't," said the first friend. "How does it work?"

"It's really simple," replied the second friend. "You just live on greens!"

What do alligators wear when they play golf?

Sportshirts with little middle - aged men on them.

"Did you know that Shakespeare was a golfer?" asked one golfer to another.

"No, I had no idea he was a golfer."

"Well, it happens to be true - I'm surprised you don't know that famous line of his."

"Which famous line is that?"

"You must know it. Haven't you ever heard of 'Putting is such sweet sorrow'?"

What's the real reason your golf pro is always telling you to keep your head down?

So you can't see him laughing at you.

A few golfers are chatting in the bar one day after a round of golf, and one of them says he sometimes takes his dog with him when he goes out to play.

"Whenever I get a bogey, my dog does a backflip." he adds.

"Really?   How extraordinary!" say the others.

"Yes, and when I get a double bogey, he does two backflips!"

"Well, that's amazing!" they say. "How does he do it?"

"Easy," he says, "I kick him twice."

A golfer named Joe was paired with one of the club's good players, and he was anxious to get some free advice. Hitting first, he swung awkwardly and topped his drive. "Do you see anything I can correct?" he asked. "I see you're standing too close to the ball," the other remarked. "After you hit it."

Two little bugs were crossing a fairway on a golf course one sunny day, when they came across a golf ball. Just as they were about to go around it, they felt the earth beneath their feet begin to shake. As they looked up they saw the golfer approaching, and started to panic. Fearing for their lives, one bug turned to the other.

"Oh my God," he squeaked, "we're going to get squashed! I don't want to die. What are we going to do?"

"We need to find a safe place where we won't get hit." said the other bug. "Quick, quick! Climb up on the ball!"

ABSOLUTELY FRIGHTFUL IRISH JOKES

Seamus was charged with deserting his wife.

"I award your wife £600 a month," said the judge.

"That's very generous of your honour," said Seamus. "I'll try and give her a few quid myself as well."

An Irishman was accused of robbing a girl, and was lined up in an identity parade. When the girl was brought into the police station to face the row of men, the Irishman pointed at her and said, "That's her."

Patrick was brought before the court, accused of selling a bottle of liquor without a licence.

"Look at this man," his lawyer said to the jury. "Do you really think that if he had a bottle of whiskey he would sell it?"

The jury took one look and found Patrick not guilty.

The Irishman was brought up before the judge.

"Why were you drunk?" the judge asked.

"I was on a train with bad companions. Four teetotallers," said the Irishman.

"They are the best company you can have," said the judge.

"I don't think so," said the Irishman, "I had a bottle of whiskey and had to drink it all by myself."

A drunk Irishman is standing, pissing into a fountain in the middle of town, so a policeman comes up to him and says, "Stop that and put it away."

The Irishman shoves his cock in his trousers and does up his zip. As the policeman turns to go, the Irishman starts laughing.

"OK. So what's so funny?" asks the copper.

"Fooled you," says the Irishman, "I may have put it away, but I didn't stop."

An Irishman who was working in an Arab country, where all alcohol was banned, was stopped at the Customs on his return from a visit home.

"What's in this bottle?" asked the customs officer, taking out a large bottle from the bottom of the Irishman's suitcase.

"That's a precious bottle of Holy Water from Lourdes that my dear mother gave me," replied the Irishman, who was a very quick thinker.

The customs officer unscrewed the top of the bottle and sniffed the liquid inside. Then he raised the bottle to his lips and took a little sip. "It smells and tastes very much like whiskey to me!" he said.

"Glory be to God!" said the Irishman. "'Tis another miracle!"

A man took his best suit to the dry-cleaners in Dublin. As he was collecting it he noticed there was a large soup stain on the front. When he pointed this out to the assistant she said to him, "You can't hold us responsible for that. It was there when you brought it in."

An Irishman stumbles out of a bar and is spied by a police constable. The constable approaches...

Constable: "Can I help ya lad?"

Man: "Yea, SSSSomebody ssstole my car!"

Constable: "Well, wheer was ya car last time ya saw it?"

Man: "It twas at the end of tiss key!" (he held up a key already in his hand).

Just then the constable notices the Irishman has his manhood out.

Constable: "Hey, ar ya aware ya expoosing yaself?"

Man: "Ohh God, they got me girl too!"

DOCTOR,
DOCTOR

The Belfast doctor's waiting room was very full. All the chairs were taken and some patients were having to stand. At first there was some conversation in the room, but as the time passed the room became even more crowded and the patients sat and waited in silence. At last an old man struggled wearily to his feet and as he turned to leave he said, "Well now, I think I'll just go home to my bed and die a natural death."

An Irish country woman went to her doctor and asked to be put on birth control pills. The doctor told her that it would be illegal in Ireland, but she said, with ten kids in ten years and still only thirty years old herself, what could she do?

The doctor suggested that she go back to the farm and cut the top off a two gallon paraffin tin. If she slept with both feet in the tin every night, she would not become pregnant.

Six months later she was back to see him again, very obviously pregnant. "I thought I told you..."

"I know you did, Doctor," the woman interrupted. "But you see he buys his paraffin in one gallon tins, so I put one on each foot."

Did you hear about the Irishman who lost his licence to practise medicine?

He was caught having sex with some of his patients. It's such a shame – he was by far the best vet in the county.

A woman goes to an Irish doctor and says, "Doctor, my husband limps because his left leg is an inch shorter than his right leg. What would you do in his case?"

"Probably limp, too," says the doctor.

The psychiatrist was advising the depressed Irishman.

"Find yourself a girl who likes to do the things you do," he said.

"But, Doctor," the Irishman protested. "What would I be wanting with a girl who likes to whistle at other girls?"

NATURAL GENIUS

What's three miles long, green, and has an IQ of 10?

The Saint Patrick's Day parade.

The cashier at this car wash in Kilburn says to this man, "Hello there! Seeing an Irishman like you here this morning has really cheered me up."

"How in the name of God did you know I was Irish?" asks the man, astonished.

"Well, we don't get many people riding motorbikes in here."

The tough guy sauntered into the dimly lit bar. "Is there anybody here called Flaherty?" he snarled. No-one answered. Again he snarled, "Is there anybody here called Flaherty?"

There were a few moments silence and then a little fellow stepped forward. "I'm Flaherty," he said.

The tough guy picked him up and threw him across the bar. Then he punched him in the jaw, kicked him, clubbed him, slapped him around a bit and walked out. About ten minutes later the little fellow came to. "Boy, did I fool him," he said. "I ain't Flaherty."

One Irish shopkeeper to another:

"How's business, Kevin?"

"Terrible, Tom, terrible. The month before last I lost £1000. Last month I lost £2000."

"So why don't you shut up shop, then?"

"But how would I make a living?"

At the start of the new school year, the teacher was getting to know all the pupils and said to one boy, "Are you Irish?"

"Yes, I am." he replied.

"What's your name?" the teacher enquired.

"Pat." he answered.

"You can't be true Irish," said the teacher. "If you were true Irish you'd say, 'Patrick'." And, turning to the boy's friend, the teacher said, "So, what's your name, then?"

"Mickrick," came the reply.

Why wasn't the Irishman worried when his car was stolen?

He got the licence plate number.

An Irish family were arguing vehemently over their eldest daughter's choice of fiancé.

"But, Mother!" she cried, "He says he'll put the whole earth at my feet!"

"You've already got the whole earth at your feet." replied her mother. "What you'll be needing is a roof over your head!"

Dominic O'Reilly went into a bank to withdraw a large sum of money.

"Can you identify yourself?" asked the teller.

Dominic pulled a mirror out of his pocket, peered into it and said, "Sure I can. That's me all right."

An Irishman was telling his friend that he thought he'd seen a ghost one night, so he picked up his shotgun and shot it. When he got up in the morning he found it was only his shirt. "What did you do then?" asked his friend.

"I knelt down and thanked God I wasn't in it".

What's the difference between an Irishman and a computer?

You only have to punch information into a computer once.

Did you hear the one about the Irishman who wanted to be buried at sea?

Six of his mates were drowned trying to dig a hole.

It was Connor and Brendan's first longhaul flight and they were heading off to Bali. They were due to land in about an hour when the pilot made an announcement. "Good afternoon, ladies and gentlemen. As you probably know, we are roughly an hour from Bali but unfortunately we've lost one of our four engines. We will therefore be landing half an hour later than scheduled but there is no need for alarm, so just sit back and enjoy the flight."

Fifteen minutes later he made another announcement. "Ladies and gentlemen, this is the Captain speaking. We have lost a second engine, but I repeat: there is absolutely no cause for alarm. We are, however, an hour behind schedule."

Ten more minutes passed before the Captain, this time sounding distinctly nervous, announced, "Ladies and gentlemen, we have now lost a third engine and we will now be arriving in Bali two hours behind schedule. I repeat, there is no cause for alarm. Please enjoy your flight but remain in your seats with your seat belts fastened."

"Mother of God!" said Connor, who had been paying close attention to the proceedings, "I hope we don't lose the last damn engine or we'll be up here all day!"

Travelling through Bali, Connor and Brendan decided to split up and do a bit of exploring on their own. When they met up again later in the evening, Connor was driving a gleaming white Porsche. "Good God!" said Brendan, "Where'd you get that from?"

"Well," said Connor, "I was walking through the town, having a bit of a look round, when suddenly this car drew up beside me, and this beautiful blonde woman offered to show me the countryside. We drove for a while and then she pulled off the road, in the middle of nowhere, took a picnic basket out of the back, and we had a great meal. Then she took off all her clothes, lay back on the blanket and told me to take whatever I wanted. So I took the car."

"Good thinking, Connor!" said Brendan. "You'd look pretty damn silly in her clothes."

How can you spot an Irish aeroplane?
   It's got an outside loo.

Did you hear about the two gay Irishmen?
   Their names were Patrick Fitzjohn and John
Fitzpatrick

What do you call an Irishman with half a brain?
   Gifted.

A travelling saleswoman from Belfast was driving through a remote, rural area in southern Ireland when her car broke down. She took to the road and eventually came across a small farmhouse. On the porch sat two brothers in rocking chairs.

"How far is it to the nearest petrol station?" she asked.

"About twenty miles, I reckon," said one of the brothers.

"Well, how far is it to the nearest hotel?"

"About thirty miles," said the other brother.

"Could you drive me there?"

"No, we don't have a car."

Despairing, the woman said, "Well, could I possibly stay here tonight? I suppose I'll have to try to hitch a ride tomorrow."

"Well now, sure you can – but you'll have to share our room."

The woman had no other choice but to agree. So before she got into the bed that night, she handed each man a condom and said, "Please wear these so I won't get pregnant."

The next morning, she left. Three months later the two brothers were sitting outside on the porch when one said to the other, "Paddy, do you really care if that Belfast woman gets pregnant?"

"Nope."

"Then how about we take these damn things off then?"

A tourist went in to a pub in Dublin, and sitting at the bar was an Irishman with the biggest dog he had ever set eyes on.

"Does your dog bite?" the tourist asked.

"No," the Irishman replied, "My dog is as gentle as a lamb."

So the tourist, reassured, went over and patted the dog and the dog nearly bit his hand off.

"I thought you just told me your dog didn't bite!" he shouted at the Irishman.

"He doesn't," came the reply. "But this isn't my dog."

Why did the Irish stop making ice?

Because the old lady who knew the recipe died.

What do you call an Irishman standing in the middle of a paddock?

A thicket.

Declan was woken by the phone ringing in the middle of the night, so he got out of bed to answer it.

"Hello?" said the caller. "Is that seven-six-double-three-double-three?"

"No," said Declan, "this is seven-six-three-three-three-three."

"Oh. Sorry to have disturbed you," said the caller.

"That's OK," said Declan. "I had to get up anyway. The phone was ringing."

Passing an office building late one night, an Irishman saw a sign that said, "Press bell for night watchman."

He pressed the bell, and after several minutes he heard the watchman clumping down the stairs. The uniformed man proceeded to unlock first one gate, then another, shut down the alarm system and finally made his way through the revolving door.

"Well," he said grumpily to the Irishman, "what do you want at this hour?"

"I just wanted to know why you can't ring it yourself."

They were sitting by the fire with steaming cups of coffee, relaxing after a hard day's work. Desmond's dog was licking his private parts, and Noel watched him enviously. "Y'know," he said, "I've always wanted to be able to do that."

"Well, it wouldn't bother me," said the ever-generous Desmond, "but I'd pat him a bit, first. He can be a bit vicious at times."

After ordering the extra large pizza at the local pizzeria, the Irishman added, "And make sure you only cut it in three pieces. I could never eat six."

An Irishman picks up a woman in a pub and asks her to come back to his place. She says, "I'd love to, but I have my menstrual cycle."

"Oh, that's OK," the man replies, "we can put it in the boot."

The hotel clerk told the Irishman that there were no more rooms with a bath, and asked whether he would mind sharing a bath with another of the male guests.

"No," replied the Irishman, "as long as he stays at his end of the bath."

An Irishman goes to the travel agency and says, "I'd like a round-trip ticket, please."

"Where to?" the assistant asks.

"Why, back here, of course."

Did you hear about the Irishman who bought an A.M. radio?

It took him months before he realized he could play it at night too.

"I wish I had a watch that tells the time," said Seamus.

"Doesn't your watch tell the time?" his friend inquired.

"No," Seamus said dejectedly, "I have to look at it."

Brendan went to a smart London restaurant with his wife and ordered an expensive bottle of wine.

"Certainly, Sir," said the wine waiter, "which year?"

"I'll have it right away," said Brendan, "if you don't mind."

Paddy was filling in the application form to join a new club.

At the bottom of the form, where it said 'Sign here,' he wrote, 'Capricorn.'

Did you hear about the Irishman who heard the country was at war?

He moved to the city.

What's the difference between a cheese sandwich and an Irishman?

A cheese sandwich is only half an inch thick.

What's the difference between a hundred cheese sandwiches and an Irishman?

Nothing.

How many Irishman does it take to change a light bulb?

Two. One to hold the bulb, and one to drink until the room starts spinning.

The Aer Lingus plane was in serious trouble over the sea.

"May day, May day, May day," radioed the Captain.

"We've got you on the screen," the air controller answered, "What's the problem? Can you give us your exact height and position?"

"Well now," replied the Captain, "I'm five foot ten and a half and I'm sitting at the front of the plane."

ABSOLUTELY
FRIGHTFUL
DRINKING
JOKES

Sitting beside Ben in the pub was the ugliest woman he'd ever set eyes on. In fact, she was so ugly that he'd refused every single one of her sexual advances.

After a couple of hours the woman turned to Ben and said, "Y'know. mishter, if I have one more drink I'm really going to feel it."

"T'tell you the truth, if I have one more drink I prob'ly won't mind!" he replied.

The drunk was staggering along the road with a large bottle of booze in each pocket, when he suddenly tripped and fell heavily to the ground.

As he was pulling himself to his feet he noticed that his trousers felt wet. He touched the wet patch with his fingers, looked blearily at them and sighed, "Thank goodnesh! It'sh only blood."

A stranger walks into a bar and the locals ask him if he wants to play a game of bar football. He says "Sure! What do I have to do?"

The locals said "Drink Beer, Piss, then Fart".

So the stranger picks up the mug and downs the beer, then takes a piss, and lets out an enormous fart.

Then the locals said, "If you can do it again, you get an extra point."

So the stranger picks up the mug again and downs his beer, drops his pants to take a piss, but before he can fart, a local shoves his large finger up the stranger's ass.

The stranger asked "What the Hell are you doing?"

"Blocking the extra point," the local replied.

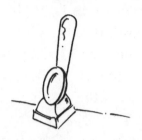

A guy walks into a bar in a high rise block late one evening, orders a beer and then walks over to admire some really strange paintings on the wall. As he is looking at the paintings another gentleman walks over and comments on the art.

"These paintings are really something, aren't they?"

"Why yes, they are quite remarkable. I have never seen anything like them before."

"You know there are other remarkable things about this bar also. You see that window over there? The way the wind currents work, if you jump out of the window, it will blow you right back into the bar. Why don't you give it a try?"

"That's impossible and crazy!"

"Look I'll show you."

The guy jumps out of the window and falls 10ft, 20ft, 30ft, 40ft, 50ft ... and then whooop! ... he stops in mid air and gets blown right back up into the window.

Now the other gentleman is dumbfounded.

"That's amazing. How did you do that?"

"I told you, it's the wind currents. Look I'll show you again."

The guy jumps out of the window and falls 10ft, 20ft, 30ft, 40ft, 50ft ... and then whooop!... he stops in mid air and gets blown right back up into the window.

This time the guy is even more impressed. He cannot believe his own eyes, but he saw it! So he decides to give it a try. He jumps out the window and falls 10ft, 20ft, 30ft, 40ft, 50ft, 60ft, 70ft, 80ft, 90ft ... and then SPLAT!

The other gentleman walks back to the bar, and the barman says,

"Gee, Superman, you can be a real asshole when you're drunk!"

Mike and John got drunk and went fishing one day. They were amazed to discover that they had caught a Genie's bottle. The Genie said he would grant one wish.

Mike said, "I wish all this water around the boat was beer."

The wish was granted and the whole lake turned into beer.

Then John said, "You've really gone and done it now, Mike! Now we'll have to piss in the boat."

A commuter approached the guard: "This morning I accidentally left a bottle of Scotch on the train. Was it handed in to the lost and found by any chance?"

"No," replied the guard, "but the man who found it was!"

DRINKS ON THE HOUSE

A travelling salesman goes into a country pub to find a great big glass jar full of £5 notes on the bar. "Put five pounds in," explains the barman. "To win the lot all you have to do is to make the donkey in the back paddock laugh."

The salesman pays up, goes out the back and whispers in the donkey's ear, and with that the donkey laughs and laughs and laughs. The salesman grabs the money and goes.

Next year the same thing happens all over again. The salesman whispers, gets the money and goes.

The next year however, the clever barman advises the salesman that the rules have all changed. This year he must make the donkey cry.

Out goes the salesman and the next thing you know the donkey is crying and sobbing uncontrollably, tears rolling off the end of his nose.

The salesman is about to leave with the money again, when the barman says to him, "That's three years in a row you've got the money. Tell me how the bloody hell did you do it?"

"Easy," says the salesman. "First two years I

simply whispered to him that my cock was much bigger than his."

"Yes" said the barman, "what about this year."

"Simple again," said the salesman, "I showed it to him."

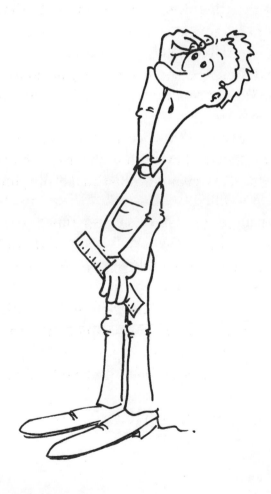

A man walks into a pub and says to the barman, "If I can really amaze you, will you give me a free drink?"

The barman, confident that he seen it all, agrees, and then is completely stunned when the man reaches into his bag and produces a piano player, less than a foot tall, who proceeds to play some pretty impressive jazz piano. The barman gives the man a drink and says, "How on earth did you do that?"

"Well," says the man, "I've got this genie who will grant you one wish. You have a go!"

The barman thinks for a bit, and then says, "Genie, give me ten thousand quid."

There's a moment's silence, then the room is suddenly filled with squid. There are squid slithering everywhere. The barman, who is clearly shocked, says, "Well I'm impressed, but I have to say that it would appear that your genie has a bit of hearing problem."

"Tell me about it," says the man, "Do you really think I asked for a ten-inch pianist?"

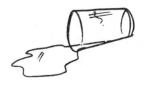

A guy walks over to a barman and offers him a bet. "I bet you £100 that I can go over to the corner of the bar and piss into this mug right here in my hand with out making a single drop. In other words in the glass and only the glass."

So, the guy goes into the corner and unzips his flies. And he's saying in his mind, 'Dick, Glass, Dick, Glass...'

So after a few minutes he starts to piss. He's pissing everywhere – on the barman, on the tables across from him, even in other people's drinks. In fact he's pissing everywhere BUT the glass!

So when he's done, the barman is standing there laughing, with piss all over his face and dripping off his chin.

The barman says, "You idiot. You just lost £100!"

And the guy says, "Well, see those guys over there? I bet them £250 that I could piss on you and you wouldn't get angry. I also said that by the time I was finished, you would be laughing!"

A length of rope was walking down the street and, feeling a bit thirsty, it popped into a pub. "Excuse me," it said to the landlord, "I'd like a pint of bitter, please."

The landlord looked at it and replied, "Aren't you a .... rope?"

"Yes, I am." said the rope.

"Well, get out of here!" said the landlord. "I'm not going to serve beer to a rope!"

Feeling rather miserable, the rope left and a little further down the street it spotted a second pub. In it went, sat down on a stool, and asked the barman for a pint.

"Hang on," said the barman, "Aren't you a ... rope?"

"Yes, but I can pay –"

"No, way!" snapped the barman. "We don't cater to ropes in this establishment."

Mortified, the rope left, but spying yet another pub it decided to try again, and this time it would not be turned down. Tangling itself up and vigorously rubbing both of its ends together, several times, it marched boldly into the pub saying loudly, "A pint of your best bitter, please landlord."

"Wait a minute" the landlord said, "Aren't you a rope?"

"No," replied the rope, "I'm a frayed knot."

A man with an enormous two foot newt on his shoulder walks into a bar and says, "A pint of lager for me, and a cola for Tiny, please."

The barman gives him the drinks and takes his money, whilst all the while staring at the enormous beast. Then he says, "Why on earth do you call him 'Tiny'?"

"Because he's my newt" the man replies.

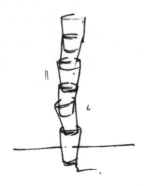

One day a man comes home from work to discover that his wife has bought him a dog. Expecting a large, lively sort of dog, he is quite happy about this until he sees that she's actually bought him a Pekinese. He takes it out for a walk anyway and bumps into a friend who is off for a drink at his local. Feeling in need of cheering up, he decides to join him. When they get to the pub, he sees a sign on the door saying, 'NO DOGS EXCEPT GUIDE DOGS'.

"Oh, bugger!" he says, looking daggers at the dog.

"Don't panic," says his friend, "We'll pretend it is a guide dog!"

"That won't work, just look at it, it's a bloody Pekinese! You don't get guide Pekinese, do you?"

"Leave this to me." said his friend, grabbing the dog's lead. He walks stiffly into the pub, up to the bar which he bumps into, slightly, and says, "Two pints of lager, please."

The landlord takes one look at the dog and says, "Sorry, mate, I can't serve you with that dog in here. We only accept guide dogs."

"But this is a guide dog," he says, trying to look as blind as possible.

"Oh, no it's not. They're all labradors or alsatians. No other dogs can learn how to do it."

"Oh my God!" shouts the friend, blindly reaching down for the dog. "What've they given me? What've they given me?"

A man walks into a bar and slaps down a pair of jump leads. The barman frowns at him and says, "Hey, don't you be trying to start anything in here."

A man walks into a bar with his pet monkey. When he gets up to the bar he sits the monkey down and asks the barman to serve his monkey a beer. The barman replies, "I am not going to serve a monkey in my bar".

After some convincing the barman agrees to give the monkey a beer. When the monkey finishes drinking the beer, he is drunk and begins to run around the bar and gets into everything that he can. Finally the monkey jumps up onto the pool table, grabs the cue ball and swallows it.

The barman, who is very upset by this time informs the customer that he will have to pay for the cue ball that his monkey has just swallowed. After some convincing, the man assures the barman that the monkey will pass the ball and he will then return it to the bar in just a few days.

As promised, a few days later the man returns with his monkey, this time on a leash, and gives the barman the cue ball back. He then asks the barman if he will once again serve his monkey a beer.

To this the barman replies, "Hell NO, the last time I did that the monkey got drunk and damn near destroyed my bar". The customer reminded the barman that the monkey is now on a leash and cannot get away from him.

After some thought the barman agrees to give the monkey a beer. The monkey sits down on the bar and begins to drink his beer. While sitting on the bar the monkey reaches over and pulls the bowl of peanuts over to him and one by one begins to eat them. Each time he picks up a peanut the monkey sticks the nut up his bottom then pulls it out and eats it. He does this several times before the barman asks, "What the hell is your monkey doing, why does he stick the peanuts up his ass before he eats them?" The man replies, "After that cue ball incident he likes to size up his meals before he eats them."

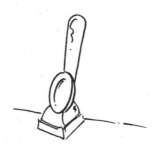

A bacon sandwich walks into a pub. He's feeling tired and run-down, and has had a dreadful day at work.

He goes up to the bar and says, "Can I have a pint of bitter, please?"

To which the barman replies, "Sorry, we don't serve food."

GREAT

DRINKING

QUOTES

Catherine Zandonella
"Time is never wasted when you're wasted all the time."

Ambrose Bierce
Abstainer: a weak person who yields to the temptation of denying himself a pleasure.

W.C. Fields
"I never drink anything stronger than gin before breakfast".

"A woman drove me to drink and I didn't even have the decency to thank her."

"What contemptible scoundrel has stolen the cork to my lunch? "

"Beauty lies in the hands of the beerholder.

"Reality is an illusion that occurs due to the lack of alcohol."

Lady Astor to Winston Churchill:
"Sir, if you were my husband, I would poison your drink."
Winston Churchill to Lady Astor:
"Madam, if you were my wife, I would drink it."

Henny Youngman
"When I read about the evils of drinking, I gave up reading."

"Life is a waste of time, time is a waste of life, so get wasted all of the time and have the time of your life."

Tom Waits
"I'd rather have a bottle in front of me, than a frontal lobotomy."

"24 hours in a day, 24 beers in a case. Coincidence?"

Oscar Wilde

"Work is the curse of the drinking classes."

Dorothy Parker

"One more drink and I'd be under the host."

Humphrey Bogart

"The problem with the world is that everyone is a few drinks behind. "

"Draft beer, not people!"

David Moulton

"Why is American beer served cold? So you can tell it from urine."

ABSOLUTELY FRIGHTFUL FOOTBALL JOKES

Our club manager won't stand for any nonsense. Last Saturday he caught a couple of fans climbing over the stadium wall. He was furious. He grabbed them by the collars and said, "Now you just get back in there and watch the game till it finishes."

Chelsea
Joe always books two seats when he goes to watch a Chelsea game. That's one to sit in and one to throw when the fighting starts.

Snow White arrived home one evening to find her home destroyed by fire. She was especially worried because she'd left all seven dwarves asleep inside. As she scrambled among the wreckage, frantically calling their names, suddenly she heard the cry: "Chelsea for the Cup."

"Thank goodness," sobbed Snow White. "At least Dopey's still alive."

Celtic/Rangers

At a Celtic v. Rangers match one season, things got a bit hairy in the crowd, with bottles being thrown by the two sets of supporters. One young spectator, stuck in the middle, was naturally rather concerned for his safety, so an old boy went to reassure him. "Don't worry, son," he said. "It's a bit like bombs in the war. One of those won't hit you unless it's got your name on it."

"That's what worries me," said the young man. "My name's Johnny Walker."

Report in a Scottish newspaper: "Celtic Park has been broken into and the entire contents of the trophy room stolen. Police are believed to be looking for a man with a green carpet."

Luton

I've started watching Luton Town. My doctor says I should avoid any excitement.

Tottenham Hotspur

A tourist is in North London one Saturday and he decides he would very much like to go to a football match, so he asks a man in the street if there are any local matches being played that afternoon.

"Well," replies the man, "the Arsenal ground is very close but they're playing away today. If you feel you really must see a match, the Tottenham ground is not that far away. You go straight down this road and you'll see two queues, a big queue and a small queue. You should go to the small queue because the big one is for the fish and chip shop."

Did you hear how Tottenham has become an all-seater stadium?

Someone gave them a 3-piece suite.

Tottenham are on the internet and they've got a new website. It's called the trophy cabinet.

A man is sitting in a pub with his Jack Russell dog one Saturday afternoon. The football results are coming up on the television in the corner, "Liverpool 2, Tottenham Hotspur 1," reads the announcer in his normal, rather sedate, voice.

Suddenly the Jack Russell dog jumps up and shouts out, "Oh, no, not again."

The shocked landlord says, "That's amazing. Why did he say that when the result was announced that Tottenham lost?"

"Because he's a Spurs supporter," the dog's owner replies.

The landlord then asked what the dog says when Tottenham win a match, to which the man replied, "I don't know. I've only had him three years."

Manchester United.

Top tip for Manchester United fans: don't waste money on expensive new kits every season. Simply strap a large inflatable penis to your forehead, and everyone will immediately know which team you support.

Q. What do you get if you see a Manchester United fan buried up to his neck in sand?
A. More sand.

Q. How many Manchester United fans does it take to change a light bulb?
A. (I) Three. One to change the light bulb, one to buy the "1998 light bulb changing" commemorative t-shirt and video, and one to drive the other two back to Torquay.
A. (II) Who cares, so long as it comes out in 4 different versions (£49.99 each), and changes twice every season?

Q. Which three league teams have swear words in their names?
A. Scunthorpe United, Arsenal and f**king Manchester United.

One afternoon an elderly man turned up at the offices of a large Manchester company.

"Good afternoon," he said, "I'm Tony Collier's uncle. I've come to ask if he can have the afternoon off so I can take him to the match."

"I'm afraid he's not here," came the reply, "We already gave him the afternoon off so he could attend your funeral."

A man walks into a bric-a-brac shop and sees an ornamental brass rat, the sort of thing women of a certain age like to put on the mantelpiece. He thinks, "that'll be perfect for my mother-in-law's birthday," so he asks the shopkeeper how much it is. "£10 for the rat, £100 for the story," replies the man.

Skip the story, thinks the bloke, and takes the rat for the tenner. He walks off down the road, but has not gone 20 yards when a rat comes up from the gutter and starts to follow him. Soon more arrive, and in a few minutes the whole street is a sea of rats, all following the bloke, who keeps walking until he comes to a cliff. He throws the brass rat over, and millions of rats follow, one after the other, plunging to certain death. The bloke then runs back to the shop...

"Aaaah", says the shop keeper, "I thought you'll be back for the story". "Sod the story, where's the brass Manchester United fan?"

Q. What's the similarity between Manchester United and a 3-pin plug?
A. They're both useless in Europe.

Plymouth

A man and his wife went to the ticket office at Plymouth football ground and, handing over a £20 note, said "Two, please."

"Thank you," said the man at the ticket office. "Would you like the goalkeeper and the centre forward, or are there two other players you'd like to buy instead?"

Derby County

...NEWS FLASH...

... Given his scoring exploits this season, it was inevitable that a major European team would come in with a seven-figure offer for Derby player, Paulo Wanchope. Unfortunately, the deal seemed doomed from the start.

... The Italian delegation, on arrival in England, got lost on the way to Pride Park. "We have never heard of Derby, they are too hopeless to play in Europe", admitted a club spokesman.

... Also, Wanchope was unable to arrange personal terms with the interested club, who could not agree to his demand that a sheep be brought in to the changing room before each match to perform sexual favours.

At a press conference, Jim Smith made no secret of his sadness at the deal falling through. "It's a great shame", said Smith. "Those seven figurines of Beatrix Potter Characters would be the best thing we've had in the trophy cabinet for years. We were even planning to claim they were Derby's prize for winning the Peter Rabbit cup, a fictitious tournament for top European sides and Derby County."...
...NEWS FLASH ENDS...

Arnold, the fanatical Derby fan always wears his replica strip, and wherever he goes people take the mickey out of him, and say he's stupid. This makes him angry, so when he next goes for his walking holiday in the Lake District, he decides not to bother. He walks through a field of sheep and sees a farmer. Feeling in need of some sexual activity he walks up and asks the farmer, "If I guess how many sheep you have, can I take one away and have sex with her?"

"OK" replied the farmer. "There are 173" said Arnold.

"That's really impressive," says the farmer. "Take your pick." Arnold chooses, and begins to walk off. The farmer shouts back, "If I can guess which team you support, can I have my dog back?"

A psychology professor decided to study the way in which different people from different parts of the country have sex with sheep. He travelled first to Wales, where he asks a farmer to explain his method: "Well, boyo, I put her back legs down my nice green wellies, grab her with me velcro gloves, and we're well away. Tidy!"

The professor tries Scotland next . "Hoots an' toots man, I put her back legs down my nice green wellies, grab her with me velcro gloves, and we're well away. Och aye tha noo!"

The professor moves on to the Lake District: "Well, I put her back legs down my nice green wellies, grab her with me velcro gloves, and we're well away. There's nowt more ti it 'yan that."

The professor is noticing a pattern developing, so he decides to try Derbyshire, and then call it a day.

He stops a bloke outside Pride Park, who happens to be our old friend, Arnold, and asks him to explain the Derby County method: "Well me duck, I put her back legs down my nice green wellies, sling her front legs over me shoulders, and that's all there is to it!"

The professor is excited to have found some regional variation, and tells Arnold that this is very different from the Scots, Welsh and Cumbrians.

"How do they do it then?" asks Arnold, and the professor explains. Arnold on hearing the explanation walks off disgusted. "What! No kissing?"

Arnold the Derby fan is walking his dog one day, when he sees an old lamp. He bends down to pick it up, and starts to rub it to clean it. Suddenly, a genie appears, and says, "I am the economy-price genie." I grant but one wish".

Arnold thinks for a while, and then says, "Make my dog Wanchope, win Crufts." The genie looks at Wanchope and says, "Don't be stupid, look at the thing. It's mangy, it's got fleas, it's got a bit missing from one ear, it limps and it smells. I might be a genie, but I'm not a miracle worker." "All right then," says Arnold, "Make Derby County win the Premier League." The genie stops for a moment, then says, "Let's have another look at that dog again."

Two Derby fans are walking along. One of them picks up a mirror, looks in it and says, "Hey I know that bloke." The second one picks it up and says, "Of course you do, you thick git - its me!"

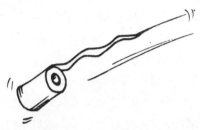

A reporter from Central News East is interviewing Jim Smith and Dave Basset. He first asks Jim what his long term plans for Derby are. Jim replies, "Well, I see us becoming a good, average Premiership team, who don't even get involved in relegation issues." The reporter then puts the same question to Harry, who answers, "I think that once we secure promotion we will be able to mount a successful challenge to the Premier League title. Once in Europe, we will carry off the European cup for the next five years." "Don't you think that's a little bit optimistic, Dave?" asks the interviewer, to which our Harry replies, "Well Jim started it."

Jim Smith was getting worried that all his players were hopeless, so he phoned up a decent manager to ask for advice. Dave Bassett explained that he got all the Forest players to dribble round cones, thus improving their close ball control. He suggested Jim try this. Two weeks later, Dave rang back to see how the Derby players were coping with the new system. When he answered the phone though Smith was still browned off. "Didn't my suggestion work?" Asked Harry. "Bloody cones! They beat us 3-0" muttered Smith.

Q. How many Derby fans does it take to change a light bulb?
A. Yeah, like they have electricity in Derby.

Arnold, the Derby fan is sent to Hell for his sins (bestiality mostly). There he meets the Devil, who asks him, "How art thou finding the eternal damnation of Hades?" "Not too bad really," says Arnold. "It's certainly warmer than Derbyshire in February, quite pleasant really."

Satan is very upset that anyone should actually enjoy Hell, so he orders his demons to turn down all the heating, until it is so cold that the very air freezes. He then goes to seek out Arnold who is smiling broadly. "What art thou doing?" asks Satan. "Is not the bitter cold chilling thy twisted soul to the bitter core?" "Yes," admits Arnold, "But I'm still happy, because this weather can only mean one thing: Derby have at last won the Premier League!"

Q. What's the best thing to come out of Derby?
A. The A52*
* Except for Cloughie. Oh, and most of the Championship team of '77-'78. But not much else.

Notts County

Last year, my aged Great Aunt, who is more than a bit senile, gave me a Notts. County season ticket for Christmas. Not wanting it, I took it down to Meadow Lane, and nailed it to the gates. A couple of weeks later, I had a change of heart, and decided that it was stupid to give something as valuable as that to any old stranger, so I went to retrieve the prized item. When I returned however it was too late. Some creep had nicked the nail.

IQ

SCORES

One of the highest paid players in the Premier division, Gary had everything going for him. He had a fancy new house in North-East London, a flash new sports car, masses of designer clothes – the lot. His only problem was that he had three girlfriends and he couldn't decide which one to marry. So he decided to give £5,000 to each woman to see what she would do with it.

The first woman bought new clothes for herself and had an expensive new hairdo, a massage, facial, manicure and pedicure.

The second woman bought a top-of-the-range VCR and CD player, as well as an expensive set of golf clubs and tennis racquet and gave them all to Gary. "I used the money to buy you these gifts because I love you," she told him.

The third woman invested the money in the stock market, and within a short time had doubled her investment. She gave Gary back the initial £5,000 and reinvested the profit. "I'm investing in our future because I love you so much," she said.

Gary considered carefully how each woman had spent the money, and then married the woman with the biggest breasts.

At the end of the day, football means not having to go to Sainsburys on Saturday.

Football is a game in which a handful of men run around for one and a half hours watched by millions of people who could really use the exercise.

Two men were at a football match and it was just seconds away from kick-off.

"Christ," said the first man, "I'm bursting for a pee, and the toilets are miles away."

"Don't worry," said the second man. "You see that bloke in front of you? Just pee up his leg."

"Are you crazy?" said the first man, "that bloke's massive."

"Oh," said the second man, "he won't notice anything."

"How do you know?" said the first man.

"Because I've just peed up yours!" said the second man.

Football players are the only people who can dribble and still look neat.

"Dad, dad!" cried Philip, as he arrived home one evening. "I think I've been selected for the school football team."

"That's good," said his father. "But why do you only think you've been selected? Aren't you sure? What position are you playing?"

"Well," replied Philip, "it's not been announced officially, but I overheard the football coach tell my teacher that if I was in the team I'd be a great draw-back."

A bad football team is like an old bra – no cups and little support.

Two boys were playing with a new football in the road outside their house.

"Hey," shouted their mother, "where did you get that football?"

"We found it," replied one of the boys.

"Are you sure it was lost?" asked the mother.

"Yes," replied the boy, "we saw some people looking for it."

They beat us five-nothing, and we were lucky to get nothing.

When I was a young boy, all the other kids insisted that I was in the football team. They said I was vital to the game. They couldn't possibly play without me. They needed me. I was the only one with a football.

A small boy was crying his eyes out at a football match. Seeing his plight, a policeman came up to him and asked what the problem was.

"I've lost my dad," cried the boy.

"What's he like?" asked the policeman.

"Beer, fags and women," said the boy.

When the manager of a Third division club started to discuss tactics, some of the team thought he was talking about a new kind of peppermint.

It was mid-way through the football season and a fourth division team were doing really badly. The manager decided to get the team together and go back to absolute basics. Picking up a football, he said, "Right, lads, what I have in my hands is called a football, and the object of the game is..."

"Hang on a minute," came a shout, "you're going too fast."

A rather dim fan arrives at a football match mid-way through the second half.

"What's the score?" he asks his friend as he settles into his seat.

"Nil-nil," comes the reply.

"And what was the score at half-time?" he asks.

The local football team were having a dreadful season. They hadn't won a game for 12 weeks and the manager was at the end of his tether. "Look," suggested a friend one evening, "why don't you take the whole squad out for a ten mile run every day?"

"What good will that do?" moaned the manager.

"Well," replied his friend, "today's Sunday. By next Saturday they'll be 60 miles away and you won't have to worry about them."

First man: "I wish I'd brought the piano to the stadium."

Second man: "Why would you bring a piano to the football game?"

First man: "Because I left the tickets on it."

A football fan lost a £50 bet on a TV football play.

He lost another £50 on the instant replay.

Q. Why do footballers play on artificial turf?
A. To keep them from grazing.

For a minute we were in with a great chance.
Then the game started.

Striker: "I had an open goal but still I didn't score. I could kick myself."

Manager: "I wouldn't bother. You'd probably miss."

Some flies were playing football in a saucer, using a sugar lump as a ball. One of them said, "We'll have to do better than this, lads. We're playing in the cup tomorrow."

A team of mammals were playing a team of insects. The mammals totally dominated the first half and at half-time were leading 39-nil. However, at half-time the insects made a substitution and brought on a centipede.

The centipede scored no less than 180 goals and the insects won the game by miles. In the dressing room afterwards the captain of the mammals was chatting to the insect captain. "That centipede of yours is terrific," the captain of the mammals said. "Why didn't you play him from the start?"

"We'd have liked to," replied the insect captain, "but it takes him 45 minutes to get his boots on."

PLAYING

AWAY

At the height of Eric Cantona's fame with Manchester United, the manager buys a Bosnian striker for their second team. Although he plays well, he goes virtually unnoticed until Eric Cantona decides to return to France, leaving a terrible gap in the side.

The manager decides to try the Bosnian out in one first team game and is delighted when he plays brilliant football and gets three goals. After the game everyone congratulates the Bosnian and the manager offers him a full contract and a huge salary.

The Bosnian is thrilled and says, "I must phone my mother to tell her the good news."

When he gets through to his mother she says, "Well, son, I have bad news for you - your father was out foraging for food and was shot dead. Your brother went out after him to try to find out what happened and to seek some recompense - he was badly beaten and had both his legs broken, and this is ALL YOUR FAULT!"

The Bosnian is shocked and says, "How is this my fault? I had nothing to do with it!" But his mother replies, "If it weren't for you, we wouldn't be in Manchester in the first place!"

There are two Bosnians playing for West Ham in an important league match. The ball comes spinning towards them but the captain, who's also well placed to receive the pass, shouts, "Mine!", and both players hit the ground.

Q. Why doesn't Pakistan have an international football team?
A. Because each time they get a corner, they open a shop.

ABSOLUTELY
FRIGHTFUL
SCOTTISH
JOKES

The American millionaire grew increasingly concerned when alcohol started vanishing from his mansion shortly after he'd hired a new butler, so he decided to confront him.

Faced with his employer's suspicions, the butler said,

"I'll have you know, I come from a long line of honest Englishmen!"

"To be perfectly frank," replied the millionaire, "it's not your English forebears which concern me but your Scottish extraction."

An Englishman, an Irishman and a Scot go out to a pub and order three pints. They each find a fly floating on the top of their mugs.

The Englishman says, "Bartender, can I have a spoon?" and quietly removes the fly from his pint.

The Irishman says, "Get out of there!" and flicks the fly away with a finger.

The Scot picks up the fly with his fingers and says, "Alright ya wee beastie. Spit it out! Now!"

An Englishman and a Scotsman were standing on a corner talking when an Irishman walked up. "You know what?" said the Irishman, "I just went into that pub over there, ordered a pint, played a round of darts and when I walked out of the pub the barman called to me to pay up. So I told him I paid when I got my pint. Well, he didn't say any more, so I got a free drink!"

The Englishman liked the idea so much he went into the pub himself and did the same thing as the Irishman. Sure enough, he came out and told the Irishman and the Scotsman that the barman had said nothing to him either.

The Scotsman decided to give it a try himself. He went in and ordered a pint. As he was chatting to the barman, the man said that two blokes had just walked out without paying. "So why didn't you say anything to them?" asked the Scotsman. "I'm not looking for trouble" replied the barman.

The Scotsman replied "Well, it's getting late, so if you'll give me my change, I'll be going home now!"

Two English ladies were discussing their holiday plans in a teashop. At the next table sat a nice little Scots lady.

"We're planning a lovely holiday in Devon this year" said the first English lady.

"Oh! You shouldn't do that" said her friend "there are hordes of Scots there. It'll be awful!"

"Dear me!" her friend replied "And where will you be going?"

"Salisbury."

"But Salisbury is simply crawling with Scots," the first lady objected.

At this point the dear little Scots lady could hold her tongue no longer. "Why don't ye both go tae hell" she suggested "There'll be no Scots there!"

A Scotsman and an Englishman lived next door to each other. The Scotsman owned a hen and each morning he would look in his garden and pick up one of his hen's eggs for breakfast.

One day he looked into his garden and saw that the hen had laid an egg in the Englishman's garden. He was about to go next door when he saw the Englishman pick up the egg.

The Scotsman ran up to the Englishman and told him that the egg belonged to him because he owned the hen. The Englishman disagreed because the egg was laid on his property.

They argued for a while until finally the Scotsman said, "In my family we normally solve disputes by the following actions: I kick you in the balls and time how long it takes for you to get back up. Then you kick me in the balls and time how long it takes for me to get up. Whoever gets up quicker wins the egg."

The Englishman agreed to this and so the Scotsman put on the heaviest pair of boots he could find. He took a few steps back, then ran towards the Englishman and kicked him as hard as he could in the balls. The Englishman fell to the floor clutching his groin, howling in agony for 30 minutes.

Eventually the Englishman stood up and said, "Now it's my turn to kick you."

The Scotsman said, "Keep the f***king egg."

Q. What's the difference between a Scotsman and an Englishman?

A. If you let a cow loose in their front gardens the Englishman will moan to his wife: "Come here quickly and help me get rid of this horrible cow that is ruining my beautiful lawn."

The Scotsman will call to his wife saying; "Come here quickly! There's a cow on the grass and it needs milking."

An Englishman, an Irishman and a Scotsman went into a pub together. The Englishman stood a round, the Irishman stood a round and the Scotsman stood around.

A condom company wanted to know what was the optimum number of condoms to put into a box, so they decided to conduct a survey.

They asked an Englishman how many he thought there should be and he said, "Seven". They asked him why he had chosen that number and he said there should be one for each day of the week.

Then the condom company asked an Irishman the same question and he answered, "Nine". They asked him why he had chosen that number and he said there should be one for every week day, two for Saturdays and two for Sundays.

Finally the condom company asked a Scotsman how many condoms there should be in a box and to their amazement he replied, "12." When they asked him why he had chosen that number he said, "January, February, March..."

An Englishman was in a restaurant in Glasgow when he suddenly suffered a severe burst of coughing and sneezing. He sneezed so violently that his false teeth flew out of his mouth and dropped on the floor, where they broke at the feet of a Scotsman.

"Don't worry, sir," said the Scotsman. "My brother will soon get you a new pair and it will be much cheaper than from an English dentist. And, what's more, he can provide a suitable set almost immediately."

The Englishman couldn't believe his luck and gladly accepted the Scotsman's offer.

The Scotsman left the restaurant and returned ten minutes later with a set of false teeth which he handed to the Englishman.

"That's fantastic!" exclaimed the Englishman, trying the teeth. "They fit perfectly. Your brother must be a very clever dentist."

"Oh, he's not a dentist, said the Scotsman. "He's an undertaker."

There is a beautiful deserted island in the middle of the Ocean where the following people are stranded:

Two Italian men and one Italian woman
Two French men and one French woman
Two Greek men and one Greek woman
Two English men and one English woman
Two Bulgarian men and one Bulgarian woman
Two Swedish men and one Swedish woman
Two Australian men and one Australian woman
Two Welsh men and one Welsh woman
Two Scottish men and one Scottish woman

One month later on this beautiful deserted island, the situation was as follows:

* The first Italian man killed the other for the Italian woman.
* The two French men and the French woman are living happily together in a 'ménage à trois.'
* The two German men have a strict weekly schedule of when they alternate with the German woman.
* The two Greek men are sleeping with each

other and the Greek woman is cleaning and cooking for them.

* The two English men are waiting for someone to introduce them to the English woman.

* The Bulgarian men took one look at the endless ocean, one look at the Bulgarian woman and started swimming.

* The two Swedish men are contemplating the virtues of suicide, while the Swedish woman keeps on bitching about her body being her own and about the true nature of feminism. But at least it's not snowing and the taxes are low.

* The Australians are all wankers, so who cares?

* The two Welsh men start searching the island for sheep while the Welsh woman gets friendly with a big banana she's found.

* The two Scottish men set up a distillery. They don't remember if sex is in the picture as things get a bit foggy after the first few litres of coconut-whisky, but at least they're happy knowing that the English aren't getting any.

Did you hear what the English, the Irish and the Scots did when they heard that the world was coming to an end?

The English all went out and got drunk.

The Irish all went to Church.

The Scots had a closing down sale.

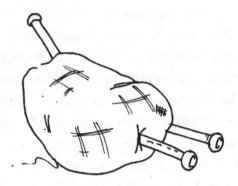

An Englishman, an Irishman and a Scotsman are standing in a field. Seeing a cow the other side of the field, the Englishman says,

"Look over there at that fine English cow."

"No, no, that's an Irish cow," exclaims the Irishman.

"No, it's not," says the Scotsman. "It's Scottish – it's got bagpipes underneath."

A Hindu, a Jew and a Scotsman are lost in the woods when they happen across a farm. They knock on the door and ask the farmer if they can stay the night. "Well, sure," the farmer says, "but I only have room for two inside, the third will have to stay in the barn."

The three men look at each other for a moment, and the Jew says, "I'll sleep in the barn." Not two minutes have passed and he comes out and says, "Oy!, I can't sleep in the barn, there are pigs there, it's not kosher."

So the Hindu says, "All is well, sahib, I will sleep in the barn." Two minutes later he comes out and says, "By the many arms of Vishnu, there is a cow in there. I cannot sleep with a cow, it would be against my faith."

The Scotsman says, "Well, that's alright, I'll take thae barn," and off he goes.

Two minutes go by when a sheep comes out......

A Scotsman and a Jew went to a restaurant. After a hearty meal, the waitress came up to the table with the bill. To everyone's amazement, the Scotsman was heard to say, "I'll pay it," and he actually did.

The next morning's newspaper carried the news item: "JEWISH VENTRILOQUIST FOUND MURDERED IN BLIND ALLEY."

There are four kinds of people that live in Great Britain:

First there are the Welsh, who pray on their knees and on their neighbours.

Next are the Irish, who don't know what they want, but they'll fight anyone for it.

Then there are the English, who consider themselves self-made men, which relieves the Almighty of any responsibility.

And last are the Scots, who hold onto their children and anything else they can get their hands on.

Give an example of perpetual motion.
A Scot running after a Jew.

During a recent international sports meeting, one of the Scottish track and field coaches was entertaining some friends and colleagues in his hotel room. As so often happens, the libations were used up before it was time to end the festivities.

After receiving directions to the nearest off licence, the Scottish coach left the party. On arriving at the off licence, he noticed that there were only three or four people waiting in the queue.

Immediately ahead of him were two men dressed in military fatigues and heavily bearded. He overheard one of them ordering several bottles of Scotch and rum. Upon being told the value of his purchases, this bearded individual told the shop assistant that he was with Fidel. Immediately the shop assistant produced a book and the individual signed for his purchases. To say that the Scotsman was intrigued would be an understatement.

The other individual in front of the Scotsman proceeded to order at least twice as much as his companion had ordered. Upon receipt of his total, he also told the assistant that he was with Fidel. The same book was brought out and the same procedure followed as had occurred with his companion.

By this time the Scotsman had decided that he was on to a good thing. He ordered numerous bottles of whisky, rum and vodka, together with cartons of cigarettes and boxes of cigars. Upon being presented with his bill, he told the assistant that he was with Fidel.

The assistant told him that he could not be with Fidel.

"Why not?" asked the indignant Scotsman.

"Because you do not have the beard and the big cigar," the assistant replied.

Pausing for only a moment, the Scotsman reached down, lifted up his kilt and proudly announced, "SECRET SERVICE!"

BRIGHT

SPARKS

The great Texan fire fighter, Red Adair walked into an Aberdeen pub. He'd just spent two weeks putting out a huge fire on a North Sea oil rig and was feeling absolutely shattered.

He ordered a pint of bitter and sat down at a table.

The Scotsman sitting next to him realised that he was an American and said:

"I've been to the States myself, ye ken! I went there last year!"

"Yeah, really!" said Red in a tired voice.

"Och aye! I spent a whole month in California. I went to this concert with the famous country singer Benny Rogers and..."

"Surely you mean KENNY Rogers!" replied Red, looking up at the ceiling.

"Aye! That's right. He sang a duet with a bonnie lass called Polly Darton."

"It's Dolly Parton, not Polly Darton" replied Red, feeling quite exasperated.

The Scotsman realized he was irritating the American, and tried to change the subject.

"Hey! Hae'n't I seen ye on the TV? Ye're famous, aren't ye?"

This made Red feel quite cheered up.

"You sure have! I'm Red Adair!" he announced proudly.

"Red Adair! the REAL Red Adair! So! Are ye still married to Ginger Rogers?"

Q. What's the difference between the New York mafia and the Glasgow mafia?
A. One makes you an offer you can't refuse and the other makes you an offer you can't understand.

Q. What do you get if you cross a Scottish mass murderer with a fish?
A. Jock the Kipper.

A Scotsman was walking along a beach when he happened to notice a bottle lying on the sand. It had obviously been washed ashore.

Thinking it might contain something of value, he picked it up and pulled out the cork.

As soon as he had unstoppered the bottle, a genie popped out in a cloud of smoke and other pyrotechnics.

"Oh, thank you for liberating me, brave sir," quoth the genie. "I have been helplessly trapped in this bottle for 40 millenia. In recompense for your kind deed, I shall grant you three wishes."

"Weel noo, laddie" replied the Scot, thinking carefully "I'd like a wee dram o' the finest whisky."

Immediately, there appeared before him a six gallon container of the very finest whisky.

The Scot immediately opened it and gulped it down, then emitted a hearty belch. Imagine his surprise when, as soon as he had put it down, it magically refilled itself to the top.

"Special feature," explained the genie, "it can never be emptied. Now what would you like for your other two wishes?"

"Why, thank ye very much," exclaimed the Scot. "I'll take two more o' the same."

A Scotsman was caught for speeding and hauled up before the judge.

"What will you take?" asked the judge. "30 days or £30?"

"I think I'll take the money," replied the Scotsman.

Sandy was only five feet tall. He attributed his lack of height to the fact that as a child in Aberdeen he was fed exclusively on condensed milk and shortbread.

WEDDED BLISS

Robbie and his wife Maggie are walking along Princes Street in Edinburgh one evening, window shopping. They stop by a jewellery shop and Maggie says, "I'd really love to have those diamond earrings."

"No problem," says Robbie. And taking a brick out of his pocket, he smashes the window and grabs the earrings. They walk off quickly but soon find themselves outside another jewellery shop, and in the window is a gorgeous, diamond ring.

"Oh, Robbie, just look at that diamond ring! I'd really love to have it," says Maggie.

Robbie looks round to make sure there's no-one around, takes another brick from his pocket, smashes the window and grabs the ring. Again they walk quickly away, and Maggie's thrilled with her earrings and her ring. A little further on they come across yet another jewellery shop and this time there is a fabulous diamond necklace in the window.

"Robbie, Robbie! Just look at that! It goes perfectly with the earrings and the ring. I really want it, in fact I must have it!"

"For God's sake, woman," says Robbie. "D'you think I'm made of bricks?"

"That Scotsman over there has 20 kids."
"Great Scot!"

A handsome young Scotsman got married. That night, after the celebrations were over and the bride and groom had left for their honeymoon night, his father was sitting down at his kitchen table, having a wee dram when the door bursts open and in comes his son.

"What are you doing here, Bobbie? You should be in bed with your bride."

Bobbie said nothing, but poured himself a large glass of whisky and sat there glumly, drinking it.

"Come on, son, tell me what the problem is. Maybe I can help you. If you really love each other there's not much that can't be sorted out."

"Well, Dad," said Bobbie, "she's a virgin."

"You'll have tae send her back then, Bobbie," said his father. "If she's nay good enough for her own family, she certainly isn't good enough for ours."

One day old Maggie asked her husband as they were going to bed, "What will become of us when you canna work any more?"

"Look out the window, woman," said

Charlie, "I own those two cottages and the shop on the corner."

"How d'you manage to buy them, Charlie, when you're on such a low wage?" she asked.

"I've been putting 50p away under the mattress each time you let me make love to you, ever since the day we married."

"Well I never!" Maggie exclaimed.

"Yes, and if you hadna been such a mean, frigid old bitch we'd hae' had two hotels and a pub," he replied.

A Scottish couple made an appointment to go to the doctor. When they were sitting in front of him he asked, "How can I help you?"

"Would you mind watching us have intercourse, Doctor?" the man replied.

The doctor was puzzled but he agreed, and the couple proceeded to have sex in his office. When they had finished they looked at him and he said, "There's absolutely nothing wrong with the way you have intercourse," and he charged them £32 for the consultation.

This happened every week for the next few weeks – the couple would make an appointment at the same time, on the same day, have intercourse, pay the doctor and leave.

Finally, one afternoon, the doctor greeted them as they came into his office and then said, "Excuse me, but I must ask you – what exactly is the problem? What is it that you are trying to find out?"

The man answered, "Nothing. She's married so we can't go to her house. I'm married too, so we can't go to mine either. The Holiday Inn charges £78. We can do it here for £32 and I can get £28 back from BUPA for a visit to the doctor's office."

The old Scotsman, McKelvie, was on his deathbed. His wife, Jean, was sitting beside him, tenderly stroking his brow and she said, "Rory, do you have a last wish at all?"

McKelvie could smell the gingerbread that his wife was baking in the kitchen and whispered, "Could I have just a wee slice of that cake that you're baking, Jean? It smells wonderful."

"I'm sorry, Rory," Jean replied firmly. "That's for after your funeral."

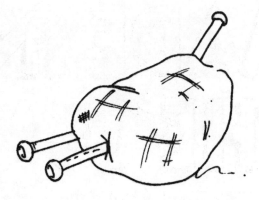

ABSOLUTELY FRIGHTFUL MADE IN THE USA JOKES

Q: Have you heard of the new Bill Clinton Computer?
A: A six-inch hard drive and no memory.

As Air Force One prepares to land, the Captain makes his customary request over the loudspeaker: 'Mr President, would you please return to the upright position and prepare to land?'

Q: What's the difference between Clinton and a screwdriver?
A: A screwdriver turns in screws, Clinton screws interns!

Did you hear that Clinton has announced there is a new national bird?
The Spread Eagle.

A reporter asked Clinton one day, 'Was Monica lying?'

Clinton responded by saying, 'No, she was on her knees.'

Q: Why does Hilary want to have sex with Bill every day at 5am?
A: She wants to be the first lady.

Dan Quayle, Frank Gifford and Bill Clinton were in a spelling contest. Unbelievably, Dan Quayle won! He was the only one of the three who knew that harass was one word.

Q: How many White House Interns does it take to screw in a light bulb?
A: None, they are too busy screwing the President.

Women in Washington DC were asked if they would have sex with the President.
86% said 'Not again.'

Clinton's team of advisors have offered the following defence...
Clinton NEVER told Lewinsky to lie in disposition! He told her to lie in THIS position...

Q: What do Monica Lewinsky and Bob Dole have in common?
A: They were both upset when Bill finished first.

Q: What is Bill's definition of safe sex?
A: When Hilary is out of town.

Q: What is the difference between Clinton and the Titanic?
A: Only 200 women went down on the Titanic.

Q: Why is Clinton so interested in events in the Middle East?
A: He thinks the Gaza Strip is a topless bar.

An American newspaper held a competition to come up with creative titles for children's books. Here are a few of the suggestions:

You Were An Accident.'

'Strangers Have The Best Candy.'

'The Little Sissy Who Snitched.'

'Some Kittens Can Fly!'

'The Protocols Of The Grandpas Of Zion.'

'How To Dress Sexy For Grown-Ups.'

'Getting More Chocolate On Your Face.'

'Where Would You Like To Be Buried?'

'Where's Godot?'

'Katy Was So Bad Her Mom Stopped Loving Her.'

'The Attention Deficit Disorder Association's Book Of Wild Animals Of North America —Hey! Let's Go Ride Our Bikes!'

'All Dogs Go To Hell.'

'The Kid's Guide To Hitchhiking.'

'When Mommy And Daddy Don't Know The Answer They Say God Did It.'

'Garfield Gets Feline Leukemia.'

'What Is That Dog Doing To That Other Dog?'

'Why Can't Mr. Fork And Ms. Electrical Outlet Be Friends?'

'Bi-Curious George.'

'Daddy Drinks Because You Cry.'

'Mister Policeman Ate His Service Revolver.'

'You Are Different And That's Bad.'

THAT
OL'
TIME
RELIGION

A new priest at his first mass was so nervous, he could hardly speak. After the service, he asked the monsignor how he had done. The monsignor said, 'When I think I'll be nervous at the pulpit, I put vodka instead of water in my glass, and if I start to get nervous I take a sip.' So the next Sunday, the new priest took his advice, and at the beginning of the service, he got nervous and took a drink. He spoke for a while, drank some, spoke some, drank some, and when he returned to his office he found a note on his door.

1: Sip the vodka, don't gulp.

2: There are ten commandments, not twelve.

3: There are twelve disciples not ten.

4: Jesus was consecrated, not constipated.

5: Jacob wagered his donkey, he did not 'bet his ass.'

6: We do not refer to Jesus Christ as 'the late J.C.'

7: The Father, Son, and Holy Ghost are not referred to as 'daddy, junior, and spookie.'

8: David slew Goliath, he did not 'kick the shit out of him.'

9: When David was hit by a rock and knocked off his donkey we don't say he was 'stoned off his ass.'

10: We do not refer to the cross as the 'big T.'

11: When Jesus broke bread at the Last Supper, he said, 'Take this and eat, for it is my body.' He did not say, 'Eat me.'

*12: The recommended grace before a meal is not
'Rubba-dub-dub, thanks for the grub, yah God!'
13: Moses parted the water at the Red Sea, he
didn't 'pass water.'
14: We don't refer to Judas as 'El Finko.'
15: The Pope is consecrated, not castrated.*

Q: Why doesn't Jesus Christ eat M and M's?
A: Because they keep slipping through the
holes in his hands!

A Jew, a Catholic, and a Mormon were talking
about the size of their families. The Jewish guy
says, 'We just had another kid. Now we have
enough for a basketball team.' The Catholic
says, 'My wife and I have enough for a
baseball team.' The Mormon guy says, 'When
I marry my next wife, I'll have enough for a
golf course.'

A BRIEF GUIDE TO
RELIGIOUS PHILOSOPHIES

Catholicism:
If shit happens, I deserve it.

Protestantism:
Shit won't happen if I work harder.

Judaism:
Why does this shit always happen to me?

Buddhism:
When shit happens, is it really shit?

Zen:
What is the sound of shit happening?

Islam:
If shit happens, take a hostage.

Hinduism:
This shit happened before.

Hare Krishna:
Shit happens Rama Lama ding dong.

Confucianism:
Confucius say 'shit.'

Rastafarianism:
Let's smoke this shit.

Jesus is preaching to a mob that is about to stone a whore: 'Let him who is without sin cast the first stone.' This old woman hobbles up, throws her stone at the whore, and the rest of the crowd follows her example. After the whore's dead, Jesus turns to the old woman and says, 'Dammit, ma! Sometimes you really piss me off!'

Q: How do you castrate a bishop?
A: Kick the altar boy in the chin!

Q: What did Jesus say just before he fell on his face?
A: Get away from here, you damn beavers!

Q: How do you get a nun pregnant?
A: Dress her up like an altar boy.

ABSOLUTELY

FRIGHTFUL

MEN AND

WOMEN

JOKES

Q: What's the smartest thing to come out of a woman's mouth?
A: Einstein's cock.

*

Q: What do you do when your dishwasher stops working?
A: Slap the bitch!

*

Q: What's the hardest part of a sex change operation?
A: Removing half the brain.

*

Q: What do you call a lesbian dinosaur?
A: Lickalotapuss.

*

Q: What's the definition of a woman?
A: Life support for a vagina.

*

Q: What do women and tornadoes have in common?
A: In the beginning they both suck and blow but you just end up losing your house.

Q: What's the definition of a virgin?
A: An ugly third grader.

Q: What's the difference between a blonde and a mosquito?
A: A mosquito quits sucking when you smack it.

Q: Why couldn't Helen Keller drive?
A: Because she was a woman.

Q: How do you get a nun pregnant?
A: You f**k her.

Q: What do you call the useless piece of skin around a vagina?
A: A woman.

Q: Why is it so hard to find a man who is sensitive, caring and handsome?
A: They already have boyfriends.

Q: Why do men name their penises?
A: They want to be on a first-name basis with the person who makes all their decisions.

✳

Q: What does a UFO and an intelligent man have in common?
A: Science can't prove either exists.

✳

Q: How many men does it take to screw in a light bulb?
A: One – men will screw anything.

✳

Q: How many men does it take to change a roll of toilet paper?
A: When it happens, we'll let you know.

✳

Q: What do you call that useless lump of fatty tissue at the end of a penis?
A: A man.

✳

Q: What's the difference between a woman and a computer?
A: What woman would accept a 3.5-inch floppy?

Q: How do you know when a man has an orgasm?
A: He rolls over and snores.

Q: When did the Jewish guy stop masturbating?
A: When his wife died.

Q: Why do women hardly ever fart?
A: They don't keep their mouths closed long enough to build up pressure.

Did you ever notice that when a man talks sex to a woman it's sexual harassment, but when a woman talks sex to a man, it's $3.95 a minute?

Q: Why do sumo wrestlers shave their legs?
A: So we can tell them apart from feminists.

OTHER BOOKS
IN THE SERIES:

THE

REALLY
WICKED
JOKE BOOK

THE

TRULY
TERRIBLE
JOKE BOOK